THE JEWISH HOLIDAY BOOK

The
Jewish Holiday
Book

by WENDY LAZAR

illustrated by MARION BEHR

DOUBLEDAY & COMPANY, INC.
GARDEN CITY, NEW YORK

Library of Congress Cataloging in Publication Data

Lazar, Wendy.
The Jewish holiday book.

Includes index.
SUMMARY: Suggests easy handicraft and cooking
projects for major Jewish holidays, the Shabbat
celebration, and Israel Independence day.
1. Fasts and feasts—Judaism—Juvenile literature.
2. Handicraft—Juvenile literature.
3. Cookery, Jewish—Juvenile literature. [1. Fasts
and feasts—Judaism. 2. Handicraft. 3. Cookery,
Jewish] I. Behr, Marion. II. Title.
BM690.L34   296.4'3
ISBN: 0-385-11426-5 Trade
0-385-11427-3 Prebound
Library of Congress Catalog Card Number 76–42342

This book is dedicated to Jodi and Kim,
who stimulated it all
and with whom I've shared happy creative hours
every day of the year.

CONTENTS

A NOTE TO PARENTS

This book is for the child, age eight through twelve, though many projects can be done in some way by children much younger. As soon as a child can hold a crayon or a paintbrush, he's ready to begin! The projects are not too difficult, not too messy, and with few exceptions, require materials you may already have in your home. Some of the activities will be a challenge for certain ages; some are quite simple. Certainly a child need not be challenged every time he's involved in a creative effort. Many of the projects here are specifically designed for younger children. This is indicated in the project with a small hand sign. If help may be needed in the kitchen, at the ironing board, or in the workshop, this is indicated by a hand-in-hand sign. Whether or not a child will be able to do part or all of a project depends on his age and ability. How much he can do without help is for you to decide since you alone know his abilities. How well he can do matters not in the least; it's the fun that counts.

In several cases it has been suggested that a project be finished with shellac. This is to make the work more permanent, but isn't always necessary. It is, however, a process best done with the help of an adult. There is another product on the market that can be used almost interchangeably with shellac. It is a non-flammable, non-toxic gloss, called Mod Podge, that is sold in craft supply stores. It is a latex glaze—milky white when wet, clear when dry. It is easy and safe to use without adult help; it dries quickly; and brushes can be cleaned in warm water.

Many crafts activities listed under one holiday can be adapted for use on another holiday. For example, the woven place mats suggested for Yom Kippur would make lovely Chanukah gifts, a Star of David is as suitable on Rosh Hashanah as it is on Israel's Independence Day and hanging mobiles and flower bouquets are ideal at any time.

Youngsters love to cook! The recipes in this book are for holiday specialties, but children can be of help in all phases of meal preparation and table setting. Their abilities improve with age, but no matter how little they do, consider it a real contribution! And just watch the older child beam as he shows you what he did—start to finish! They'll burst with pride when you tell aunts, uncles, and cousins by the dozens of their part in the holiday preparations.

A child will need guidance and sometimes the help of an older person. He will also want you standing by to provide attention, encouragement, and final hurrahs. You'll all have a wonderful time!

I extend special thanks to my two imaginative daughters, Jodi and Kim, who helped with the research, and to my husband, Martin, who has encouraged and admired our co-operative, creative efforts. Special acknowledgment goes to Marion Behr, who has proven again that working with her is a joy.

Shabbat

One nice thing about Shabbat is that while all our other Jewish holidays come once a year, this one comes every week. It starts on Friday evening. In many Jewish homes, Mother lights two candles, and Father says a prayer over the wine and the braided bread, called *challah*. Then everyone has dinner. On Friday night or Saturday morning, you may go to synagogue or read or play quiet games, visit relatives, and sing Shabbat songs. In some families on Saturday evening, Father lights the Havdalah candle. It is a special one of different colors with many flickering lights. He also opens a Besamim box filled with sweet-smelling spices, such as cinnamon or cloves. The Havdalah service prepares the family for the rest of the workday week. It helps them leave Shabbat behind. The fragrance of the spices is like the spirit of Shabbat that carries over into the rest of the week. Shabbat is a day of rest and peace, and so when we meet people on that day we say in Hebrew, "*Shabbat Sholom.*"

SHABBAT CANDLESTICKS

1. For each candlestick, roll a piece of clay between your hands until it forms a ball the size of a small orange. Press it down on the work table to flatten the bottom. With your thumb, press a hole in the center about an inch deep. Put a Shabbat candle in the hole for proper fit. Make designs with a stick. Let the clay harden, then paint.

2. Fancier candlesticks can be made from two flat-bottomed juice glasses. On the outside, stick on beads, painted pasta, or buttons with white glue. What's even more fun—and definitely tasty—is to lick gum candies and press them onto the glass in various designs. Drip some hot candle wax into the bottom of each glass, and while still hot, set in the Shabbat candles. You can also buy a wax product in candle stores that firmly holds a candle in any oversize container.

CHALLAH COVER

Use a man's handkerchief for this. Draw a Jewish symbol on the cloth. Color it in with wax crayons. Press hard so the colors are dark. When this is done, place the cloth on a thick pad of newspaper. With the picture face down, go over it with a hot iron. The colors will melt slightly into each other and get lighter. If needed, outline the design with a permanent color felt-tip marking pen. When the cloth gets dirty, it can be washed in the washing machine since the design has been made permanent.

NAPKIN RINGS

1. To make the napkin rings, use tongue depressors, which can be bought at drugstores. For each one soak a tongue depressor in water until it can be bent, then carefully fit it around the inside of a small drinking glass. Let dry. Remove it from glass. Decorate with acrylic paint, then glue on glass beads, fancy buttons, or shells.

2. Empty cores from cellophane tape rolls make strong napkin rings. They can be decorated with colored plastic or cloth tape or trimmed with small beads that can be bought at craft supply or dime stores. The tape and beads come in many colors, so you can use just one or make designs with two or three colors. Household cement will hold the beads on the plastic core but it's a delicate job so you may want some help.

HOLIDAY GUESS

Think of a Jewish holiday. Give one hint about it to the other players. Let everyone have a turn. There are lots of holidays and each can be used more than once. Here are some ideas for you.

We spin a four-sided top.   (*Chanukah*)
We eat outdoors in branch-covered booths.   (*Sukkot*)
The holiday comes every week.   (*Shabbat*)
The Torah is carried around the synagogue.   (*Simchat Torah*)
Trees are planted.   (*Tu Bishevat*)
We use loud noisemakers and stamp our feet.   (*Purim*)
We eat *charoses*.   (*Passover*)
We are reminded of the warrior Bar Kochba.   (*Lag Ba'Omer*)
The first two days of the Jewish month, Tishri.   (*Rosh Hashanah*)
May 14, 1948.   (*Israel Independence Day*)
Symbols of this holiday are the *lulav* and *etrog*.   (*Sukkot*)
The Megillah is read.   (*Purim*)

CHALLAH

4½ to 5½ cups unsifted flour
2 tablespoons sugar
1½ teaspoons salt
1 package active dry yeast
⅓ cup soft margarine

1 cup very hot tap water
4 eggs, room temperature
1 teaspoon cold water
¼ teaspoon poppy seeds, if you
   like them

1. In a large bowl mix together 1¼ cups flour, sugar, salt, and undissolved yeast. Add margarine. Gradually add very hot water. Beat 2 minutes on medium speed of an electric beater. Scrape down the sides with a spatula occasionally.

2. Add 2 more cups of flour, 3 eggs, and 1 egg white. (For directions on how to separate the yolk and the white, see homemade Cookie Paint on page 59.) This will make a thick batter. Stir in enough additional flour to make a soft dough.

3. Turn out on a lightly floured board. To knead dough, push it down and away from you with the heels of both hands. Roll it back and push it away again. Keep rolling, pushing, and turning the dough until it is smooth and elastic, about 15 minutes. Roll it into a ball. Place dough ball in a well-greased bowl. Turn dough upside down to grease top, too.

4. Cover with a clean towel. Let rise in a warm place, free from drafts, until double in size—1 to 1½ hours.

5. Punch dough down. Turn onto lightly floured board. Divide in half.

6. Divide one half into three fairly equal pieces. Using your hands with the dough on the board, roll each of the three pieces into strips, about 12 inches long. Fasten the three together at one end by pinching the dough. Now braid the dough into a twisted loaf. To braid, fold the outside strip over the center strip each time, first from one side, then from the other. When braided, pinch together open ends to close. Prepare the other half in the same way.

7. Place loaves on a large greased baking sheet. Beat together the one remaining egg yolk and the cold water. Brush yolk mixture on loaves. Sprinkle on poppy seeds.

8. Let the dough rise, uncovered, in a warm place free from drafts until double in size, 1 to 1½ hours.

9. Bake at 400° F. for 30 minutes or until golden brown. (The smell of fresh bread is delicious!) Remove from baking sheet and cool on wire racks.

This recipe makes two challahs. If that's too much, put one in the freezer for another time.

✋ BESAMIM BOX

Besamim are the spices that are used in the Havdalah ceremony on Saturday night.

To make this spice box cover a large match box with bits of colored construction paper, adhesive-backed paper, plastic or cloth tape, ribbon, or paint. The inside box will slide out to receive the spices.

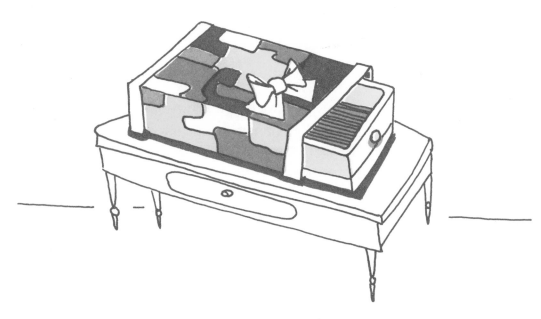

Rosh Hashanah

Our calendar year starts on January 1, but our Jewish year begins in September or October on the first two days of the Jewish month Tishri. Rosh Hashanah is the Jewish New Year.

It's a time to send New Year cards to friends and relatives. Families go to synagogue together and listen to the blowing of the shofar. The shofar is a ram's horn that calls the Jews together now—just as it did when Moses brought the Jews news of the Ten Commandments. When blown the shofar sounds something like T'KEE-AH! It is blown three times during Rosh Hashanah. This is a special time for thinking about oneself and how one has behaved toward others. It's a serious holiday but a happy one, as well. It's a day of family togetherness, a beautifully set dinner table, and good holiday food. Many families eat honey cake or apple slices dipped in honey in the hope that the new year will be full of good, sweet things.

NEW YEAR CARDS

There are so many ways to make cards it is difficult to be selective. Here are just a few possibilities.

1. Let's start with an inking pad. Place water-color paint in a shallow dish. Make a pad of several thicknesses of paper toweling and place it over the paint. Let the paint soak through the pad. Press the items for inking on the pad, then print on paper.

Leaves, corks, spools, bolts, nuts, screws, sponges, clothespins, or any small object of unusual shape having one flat side can be used for printing patterns. Also, different shapes can be cut from the ends of potatoes, carrots, corks, and erasers. A hard vegetable, like carrots, celery, radishes, potatoes, and turnips, or those with a hard middle, like mushrooms, Brussels sprouts, and cauliflower can also be used. Try an onion, too. Cut one onion lengthways and another one across and see what patterns they print. To cut a vegetable, always hold it down on a hard, flat surface and cut down with a knife. Remember to keep your hands away from the knife blade!

2. Cut a piece of colored paper about 6 inches wide and 5 inches high. Then cut a piece of white paper a little smaller, about 5 inches wide and 4 inches high. Glue the white sheet to the colored paper so a colored border goes around the edges. Design a pretty border with crayons or felt-tip pens. Write your message and sign your name on the white paper.

3. Still another way: cut a piece of colored paper about 6 inches wide and 5 inches high. Stars of David and shofars may be cut from aluminum foil and glued on this card.

NEW YEAR BINGO

For each player, have one or two pieces of paper 6 inches square. With a ruler, draw three lines 1½ inches apart across and down a total of six lines. Measure from outside edges. There will be sixteen 1½-inch squares when done. On each paper write—in any order—the names of eight Hebrew months and eight English months. On twenty-four smaller pieces of paper write the names of the twenty-four Hebrew and English months:

TISHRI	NISAN	JANUARY	JULY
CHESHVAN	IYAR	FEBRUARY	AUGUST
KISLEV	SIVAN	MARCH	SEPTEMBER
TEVET	TAMMUZ	APRIL	OCTOBER
SHEVAT	AV	MAY	NOVEMBER
ADAR	ELUL	JUNE	DECEMBER

Mix up the papers in a bowl.

To play, give each player a "Bingo" card and some buttons or pennies. Draw the name of a month from the bowl and call it out. If it's on a card, the person with that card puts a button or penny over the name. The first player with a line of pennies up, down, across, or diagonally calls out "Bingo" and wins the game. Maybe he also wins the pennies?!

24

WOODEN TRIVET

Hot *tzimmes* on a colorful hot plate!

Ice cream sticks or craft sticks for this project are sold in dime stores or in hobby shops. With white glue, attach five of these sticks at right angles to five other craft sticks, so that the lines are perpendicular to each other as in the capital letter L. It will form a square of crossed wooden sticks. On the underside around the edges, glue colored beads to make a stand. On top, where the sticks are joined, decorate with poster or acrylic paints. If a shiny coating is desired, finish with shellac, following directions on the can. (Do not use Mod Podge for this—it is a plastic glaze, and is not heat resistant.)

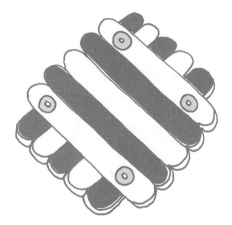

WIPABLE PLACE MATS

When there are special dishes on the table, why not have special mats beneath them?

1. Flannel-backed oilcloth makes a sturdy place mat. Cut colored oilcloth about 18 inches wide by 12 inches high. Trimming the edges with pinking scissors will give you a pretty zigzag edge. The mats can then be decorated with various colored plastic or cloth tapes. That's all there is to it!

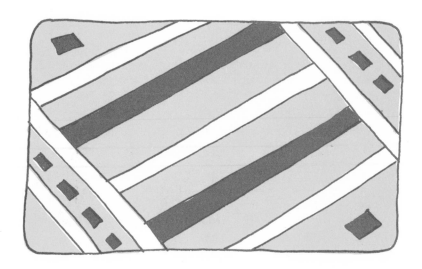

2. Cut a piece of colored tissue paper 15 inches wide by 12 inches high. Fold it several times in quarters, eighths, in any way you wish. Cut designs in the folded paper. Smooth out the paper and place it over a piece of construction paper of the same size in a contrasting color. Place both pieces between two slightly larger sheets of waxed paper. Run a warm iron over them to seal.

APPLE CUP AND HONEY

Honey is a symbol of sweetness and it is used at Rosh Hashanah as a wish for "sweetness in the New Year." One popular dish is apples and honey. This is easy enough for a very young cook.

Wash and core one apple and hollow out part of the inside. Fill the center of the apple with honey. Wash and core a second apple, slice it in sections, then place it around the apple cup.

HONEY FRUIT CAKE

⅔ cup butter or margarine,
   room temperature
1½ cups honey
3 eggs
1 tablespoon baking powder
1 teaspoon cinnamon

1 teaspoon ground cloves
½ teaspoon salt
2⅔ cups unsifted flour
½ cup milk
2 cups raisins

1. Heat oven to 325° F.

2. Grease well two loaf pans—9½ by 5½ by 3 inches.

3. Beat the butter until it becomes soft and fluffy; add honey. Add eggs and mix well.

4. Add baking powder, cinnamon, cloves, and salt. Add flour alternately with milk.

5. Beat well after each addition. With a wooden spoon or spatula, stir in raisins.

6. Pour batter into pans. Bake at 325° F. for 50 to 55 minutes.

Yom Kippur

Yom Kippur is a time for thought and prayer when we think about the things we've done right, the things we've done wrong, and how we can do better. We remember some of our arguments with brothers and sisters or how we forgot to help clean up our books and toys. Then we think of ways to be a better person, a better member of the family, and a better friend. Mothers, fathers, and older brothers and sisters may go without food that day. Families go to synagogue, and in their prayers, promise to do good deeds in the year ahead. In most synagogues, Yom Kippur begins with a song called "Kol Nidre." Kol Nidre are words meaning promises. The melody of the song is very beautiful. At the close of this day, the shofar is again sounded in the synagogue. It is a hopeful note for a promise of happiness in the coming year. T'KEE-AH!

WOVEN PLACE MAT

It might be nice to have a specially made place mat on the table under the candles or the flowers.

1. Start with a piece of white paper measuring 12 inches by 9 inches. This will be the weaving sheet. Fold it in half to measure 12 inches by 4½ inches. Rule a 1-inch border on the three open sides. Leaving a 1-inch margin at top and bottom of the paper, draw lines with a ruler across the width of the paper ½-inch apart. There will be twenty-one lines drawn. When cut with a scissors, each slit will measure 7 inches in length when paper is unfolded. Cut six strips of colored paper to measure 1 by 12 inches. Take one of the strips and slide it over and under the slats of the weaving sheet, until it has been woven across the full width of the sheet. Push that woven strip up to the top of the sheet, then begin again with the next one. This time weave in the opposite way. Where it went under with the first strip, it now goes over with the second. Each time push the woven strip up against the strip that came before. When completely woven, tape the strips down along the back edges of the 1-inch margin, so they won't get loose. To waterproof and strengthen this mat, cover the entire face of it with transparent tape, clear contact paper, or Mod Podge.

2. For a mat that is easier and quicker to make, cut the slits farther apart and the strips wider. For example, you could make eleven slits 1 inch apart on the weaving sheet with three 2-inch strips.

3. A fabric mat can be made in the same way, though when it is completed the cloth strips should be sewn down along the edges.

THE TEMPLE

Because he was a man of peace, King Solomon was permitted to build the Temple of Jerusalem. It took seven years and more than 180,000 laborers to complete the job. Descriptions of their work are in the Bible. The Temple was a rectangular building of three areas: Court, Altar, and Ark. The inner area, which contained the Ark, could be entered only by the High Priest, and by him only on Yom Kippur.

The blocks for this young builders' activity can be made many days or weeks before Yom Kippur and used throughout the year. Collect assorted size boxes from dried foods, shoes, jewelry, gifts, clothes, or soaps. Tape them closed. Paint them with poster paints. If you like, you can also glue on magazine pictures or attach gummed labels. Let dry completely. Be sure to add on extra decorations in only one thin layer so each box will lie flat.

Now build the Temple—or anything else you might like to create!

FLOWER VASE

Cut off the top of a milk or juice container. Cut a piece of aluminum foil a little longer and a little wider than is needed to go around the box. Spread a light coat of glue over the box and press the foil around the box. Tuck the top edge inside. Glue down the open edge. With an ordinary lead pencil draw designs over the foil and, surprisingly, it will take on the appearance of an engraved silver vase.

It is also possible to attach bits of colored paper to the box with white glue. If a shiny coating is desired, cover with Mod Podge.

Fill with real flowers, paper flowers, or artificial flowers. This vase will make a pretty table decoration during the holidays.

APPLE COMPOTE

This is a simple dessert to serve at dinner after the Yom Kippur fast.

6 apples
4 tablespoons sugar
2 cups water
1-inch cinnamon stick or
   3 to 4 tablespoons cinnamon candies

1. Wash, quarter, core, and peel apples.

2. Make a syrup of sugar and water, cooking them over low heat. Add the cinnamon.

3. Add apples to hot syrup. Cook the apples in the syrup until tender, about 15 minutes.

4. Serve hot or cold with syrup in sauce dishes. Makes 4 servings.

Sukkot

Five days after Yom Kippur comes Sukkot. It's a thanksgiving celebration of the harvest when we build branch huts or booths called *sukkahs*. A long time ago, the Jews really had to live in branch huts after they left Egypt as slaves and wandered in the desert for many years.

סכה

Sukkah in Hebrew is written above. As the pictures of the Hebrew letters tell us, the sukkah may have 2½, 3, or 4 walls. It is a temporary structure to represent the dwellings that the Jews set up in the desert. Sometimes a family builds a sukkah in their back yard. The roof is covered with branches so you can see the stars from inside.

Children can decorate the sukkah with fruits, vegetables, and flowers. Families eat their meals in it during the week. It's fun! It smells of pine branches and oranges and apples.

There are special services in the synagogue, when palm branches are waved and yellow, sweet-smelling citrons are held. A citron is cousin to the lemon and is called *etrog* in Hebrew. The palm branches are *lulav*. Both are used to represent the fruits of Israel during the festival of Sukkot.

MINIATURE SUKKAH

Turn a sturdy shoe box on its long side. Cut away the top and strips of cardboard from the sides and back, leaving enough to keep it standing upright. Cut out fruits and leaves from colored paper. Gather leaves, twigs, and acorns. Place them on top of the box. Glue paper fruits and leaves to the back and sides of this miniature sukkah. It will make an attractive holiday decoration.

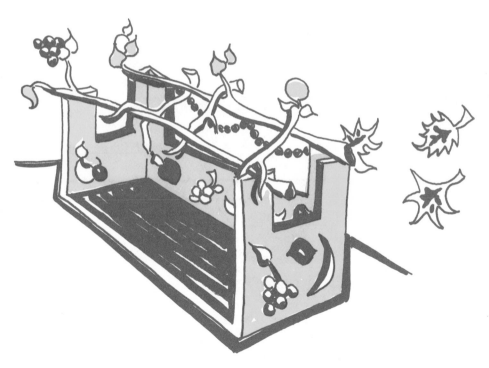

HARVEST CART

Take a small box (a children's shoe box would be perfect) and decorate it with crepe paper or cover with poster paint. Glue on cardboard circles for wheels. Add a cardboard wagon handle, or attach handle and wheels with brass fasteners. You can punch holes in the cardboard with the point of a scissor. Carefully, please! Fill with cutout paper fruits or, better yet, for a special holiday centerpiece on your table, fill with real fruits, or clay-dough fruits, if the cart is strong enough to hold them.

CLAY-DOUGH FRUIT BASKET

Mix together 4 cups of flour and 1 cup of salt, then add 1½ cups of water. Mix with spoon, then with hands. Knead dough on generously floured board for 10 minutes until dough is smooth. If it's still sticky, knead in a small amount of flour. If too crumbly, knead in a small amount of water. Work with half the clay-dough at a time. Keep the unused portion in a plastic bag in the refrigerator.

On a sheet of aluminum foil, roll out the dough into a ½-inch-thick slab. Cut out fruit shapes or roll between palms to make balls or coils. Form balls into fruit shapes and place on foil-covered cookie sheet. Suggestions for fruit shapes are: apples, oranges, bananas, cherries, strawberries, grapes, cantaloupes, watermelons, pears, plums, peaches, lemons, limes, and pineapples. If joining surfaces, as when putting the stem on an apple, moisten dough on the touching surfaces.

Bake shapes at 325° F. for 1 to 2 hours till hard. Small, thin fruits will require less baking time than large, thick fruits. Check for hardness by trying to stick a toothpick in or pressing with a wooden spoon. The fruits get very hot when baking. Use a pot holder! Let shapes cool.

Decorate with felt-tip markers, water colors, or acrylic paints. When dry, cover completely with two or three coats of clear nail polish, letting it dry about 1 hour between coats. This helps the clay-dough harden and keeps the paint from coming off. Mod Podge may also be used.

When completed, put the fruits in a pretty bowl or wicker basket and use as a holiday decoration. (If you have clay-dough left over after this project, just refrigerate it in a plastic bag for use at a later time.)

CARROT RAISIN SALAD

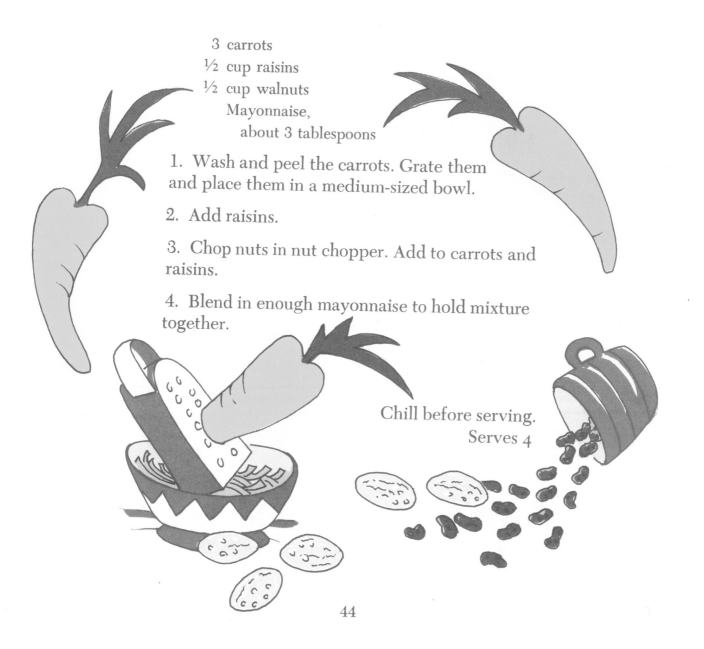

3 carrots
½ cup raisins
½ cup walnuts
Mayonnaise,
about 3 tablespoons

1. Wash and peel the carrots. Grate them and place them in a medium-sized bowl.

2. Add raisins.

3. Chop nuts in nut chopper. Add to carrots and raisins.

4. Blend in enough mayonnaise to hold mixture together.

Chill before serving.
Serves 4

SEED MOSAICS

This project is good for the
whole family, because it takes a
long time to complete—especially
if you choose small seeds and a
big design.

There are many designs you can "paint" with seeds, rice,
barley, and dried peas and beans. Try a fruit arrangement
for the holidays. Draw an arrangement of fruit—
watermelon, oranges, and lemons—on a piece of stiff
cardboard, the smooth side of a corrugated board, or
plywood. Shallow dishes are handy for keeping the materials
separate. Do one seed grouping at a time. Fill in the sections
with white glue first, a small area at a time. By spoon or
hand, place the seeds or beans in the appropriate sections.
Try to fill in all spaces, including the background. When
completed, if a shiny coating is desired, give the entire
mosaic two coats of shellac. Allow about 2 hours between
coats. Shellacking is best done in a workbench area on old
newspapers. One coat of Mod Podge will also work.

Here are some seed ideas for the fruit arrangement:

WATERMELON: The flesh of the melon can be split or whole red kidney beans. Scatter a few pits, using sunflower seeds. The rind can be black poppy seeds.

LEMONS: Yellow split peas.

ORANGES: The small round orange seeds found in bird seed.

BACKGROUND: Green split peas.

If you would like to make your own seed and bean mosaic design, simple ones are best, here are color guides to help you:

RED: red kidney and lentil beans

ORANGE: yellow split peas; orange seeds in bird seed; popcorn kernels

YELLOW: mustard seeds; yellow split peas; popcorn kernels

WHITE: lima, navy, marrow, black-eye and white kidney beans; pumpkin and sesame seeds; white rice

GREEN: green split peas; green soybeans; shelled pumpkin seeds

BROWN OR TAN: red kidney, lentil, and pinto beans; caraway, celery, and dill seeds; brown rice; barley

BLACK: poppy and sunflower seeds; black beans

Each varies in shade, size, and texture, which must be considered when choosing the right one. All are available in most supermarkets.

SUKKOT MOBILE

Three wire coat hangers hooked together as the picture shows will make a simple mobile. Cut from construction paper: fruits, flowers, a Star of David, vegetables. Decorate with felt-tip pens, silver foil, or paper cutouts. Hang them with the string from hangers. Tie the strings loosely around the hangers, so the objects can be moved easily when adjusting the balance.

HANGING IN MY SUKKAH

The first player begins by saying, "Hanging in my sukkah is a lemon." The second one repeats what the first said and adds the name of another fruit or vegetable, such as, "Hanging in my sukkah is a lemon and an apple." The third repeats both and adds his own—"Hanging in my sukkah is a lemon and an apple and a banana." And so it goes. If a player forgets something or gets the order wrong, he is out of the game. The last one left is the winner.

Simchat Torah

The last day of Sukkot is Simchat Torah. This is a holiday in honor of the Torah, the first five books of the Bible which tell the early story of the Jews. On this day the last chapters of the Torah are read, and immediately after, the first chapter of the first book of Genesis is begun again. This is a very happy time. The Torah is carried around the synagogue as the children parade up and down the aisles, singing and carrying flags or candles in hollowed-out apples. After the marching, the children are given nuts and candies.

PAPER TORAH

Plastic or paper drinking straws can be used for handles. Cut
a strip of white shelving paper about 18 inches long. Its height
should be 3 inches shorter than the height of the straws.
Tape one straw to each end of the paper. Tightly roll the
Torah up and tie with a ribbon. From colored construction
paper, cut a strip of paper to fit around the Torah. Draw a
design on it using paint or felt-tip pen. If desired, fringe
the bottom with scissors. Place the cover around the Torah,
overlapping the edges. With a double-edged masking tape or
cellophane tape, close it at the back.

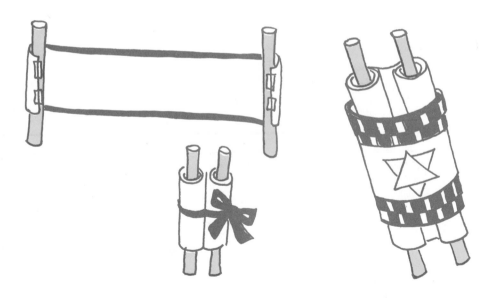

PICTURE COLLAGE

A collage is a picture of different kinds of materials glued together to form a design. You can use as many items as your imagination allows. Here are some examples: colored paper, color chips from paint store color charts, pipe cleaners, straws, beads, macaroni, cloth scraps, tinfoil, canceled stamps, feathers, yarn, ribbon, wooden ice cream spoons, seashells.

Paint a plywood board a color you like. Plan your design. When the paint is dry, draw a Simchat Torah picture in outline—apples, flags, or whatever you like best. Fill the outline with a thick coat of white glue. Place the bits and pieces of your selected materials while the glue is still wet. Allow the glue to dry completely. You can give it a shiny coating with Mod Podge. This will make a pretty holiday decoration for your home.

PLAIN AND FANCY FLAGS

1. Fold a piece of paper 8½ inches by 11 inches into four equal parts in half on the length and in half on the width. Cut away the bottom right quarter. The section above that will be the flag. Color it with any good design for Simchat Torah. It can be cut into different shapes. Press hard as you roll the large rectangular section toward the flag. If pressed down well, this handle will not unfold.

2. For a larger flag, take a piece of construction paper and cut it to a simple flag shape. Color it with any design. Then glue or staple it to a narrow dowel or stick.

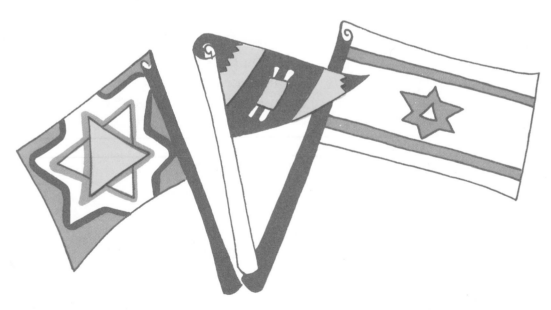

FLAG IT DOWN

Cut enough drinking straws in half so there will be a half straw for each player. From colored tissue paper, cut one "flag"—a 3-inch square—for each player. Ask everyone to sit at one side of the room. Make a finish line with a chair or low table at one end of the room. At the end of the room opposite the finish line, place the flags on the floor—divided up like the teams. If there are four players each on two teams, put four flags in two piles. Explain that the object of the race is to move each flag from the starting line to the finish line without touching it with your hands. Show how to do this by placing one end of the straw in your mouth. Bend down and pick up a flag by inhaling through the straw. Hold your breath, walk across the room, and put down the flag at the finish line. Divide the players into teams. Give everyone a straw. (Be sure that young players know how to inhale through a straw.) Explain that they may touch the straws but never the flags. If a flag drops, the player may start again wherever he is. When the first player of each team gets his flag to the finish line, the second player does the same, then the third, and the fourth. And so it goes till the first team to get their flags to the finish line wins the race. Let the players of the winning team play each other until there is one grand winner.

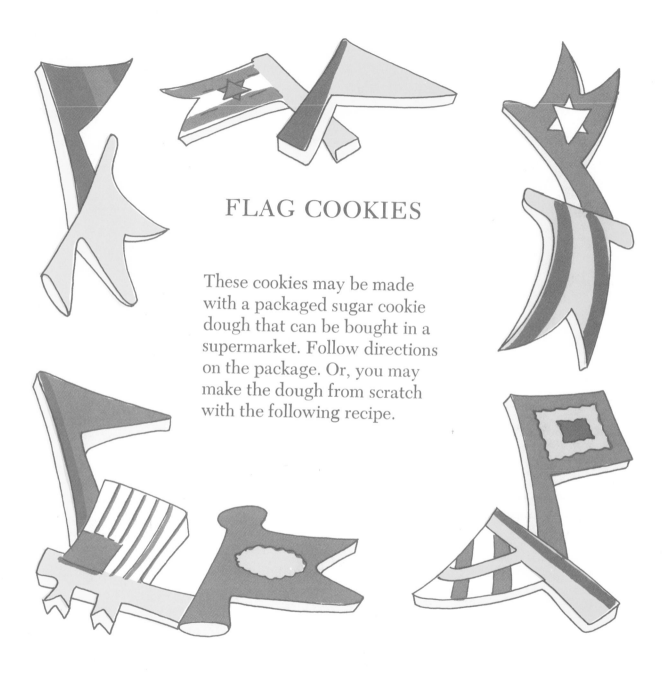

FLAG COOKIES

These cookies may be made
with a packaged sugar cookie
dough that can be bought in a
supermarket. Follow directions
on the package. Or, you may
make the dough from scratch
with the following recipe.

½ cup butter or margarine, room temperature
½ teaspoon vanilla
¾ cup sugar

1 egg
2 tablespoons milk
½ teaspoon salt
2¼ cups unsifted flour

1. Cream butter and vanilla until light and fluffy. Add sugar gradually. Beat it in well. Add egg and beat well. Beat in milk. Add salt. Add enough flour so that when the dough is touched lightly with an unfloured finger, it comes away clean.

2. To make rolling easier, refrigerate the dough until firm. That's about 2 hours in the refrigerator or 15 minutes in the freezer.

3. Dust a bread board and rolling pin with flour. Roll out the cool dough about ¼ inch thick. Cut into flag shapes with a knife. Place on ungreased cookie sheets.

4. Now it's time to "paint" the flags (see page 59).

5. After painting, bake at 350° F. for about 15 minutes or until barely browned at edges.

COOKIE PAINT

To make the "paint," you need 2 eggs and new, unused paintbrushes. First you must separate the egg yolks from the whites. With each egg: crack it by tapping it at the center with a knife or against the side of a sturdy bowl. Hold the egg in an upright position over a bowl. With your thumbs, widen the crack by pulling the edges apart until the eggshell is broken in halves. Some of the egg white will slip into the bowl. Carefully transfer the yolk from one half eggshell to the other, letting the egg white slip out but being careful not to break the yolk or allow it to fall into the bowl. Also, try not to get the thick, white membrane in with the yolk. It will make your paint lumpy. When yolk and white are separated, divide the egg yolk among four custard cups or paper cups. (Use whites the next morning in scrambled eggs.) Make each cup a different color—red, blue, green, yellow—by adding a few drops of food coloring. Mix well with a paintbrush. If paint thickens, just add a bit of water to it. Clean brush with warm water before putting it in a new color. Now you're ready to paint designs on the flag cookies (see page 56). Have fun!

Chanukah

Chanukah is a happy holiday that lasts for eight fun-filled days. There are singing, laughter, games, gifts, stories, and bright candles—all celebrating a great victory of the Jewish people under the leadership of Judah Maccabee. It was a very long time ago. When oil was needed to light the menorah in the Temple of Jerusalem, just a little was found—only enough for one night. But by a miracle, it burned for eight days and nights while the Jews celebrated the rededication of the Temple. Chanukah means "dedication." We use a menorah with nine places: one for each of the eight nights and one called the *shamash*, which is used to light the others. One candle is lit the first evening, two on the second evening, three on the third, and so on until all eight candles are glowing on the eighth evening. Presents are given to the children—maybe a toy, a book, or Chanukah *gelt*. But why not surprise your family with gifts for them? Gifts you've made yourself! Ideas are here for all ages. You might want to start creating several weeks in advance. It's part of the fun of Chanukah!

JUDAH MACCABEE

Start with an empty 1-pound coffee can and cover it with white paper. Glue on eyes and nose, cut from colored paper or felt, and draw mouth. Cut an arm piece from white paper long enough to go around the cylinder with room to spare. Draw and cut out a Star of David. Cut out a spear, hat, and shield from colored paper. Glue star to shield and hat to top of cylinder. Place spear in one hand so bottom of spear is even with the bottom of the cylinder. Fold hand around spear and glue. Glue shield to free hand.

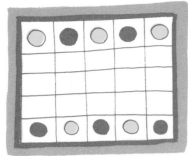

MACCABEE LINE-UP

This game requires an even number of players—two, four, six, or eight. For each two players, cut a piece of paper so it measures 7½ inches square. Using a ruler, mark off twenty-five 1½-inch-square boxes. That's five to a line in any direction. For each game, ten "Maccabees" are needed. They may be buttons, poker chips, or large beads, but there must be five of one color and five of another. Pennies and nickels may also be used. Give each player five Maccabees, all the same color. He lays them down as shown in the first picture. The object of the game is to move the men until one player has all of his in a straight row. Players take turns moving, one square at a time. They make one move at a time—forward, backward, sideways, in either direction, or kitty-cornered. Men may not be jumped as in checkers. The winning player may get his Maccabees into a straight line up, down, crosswise, or from one corner of the board to the other.

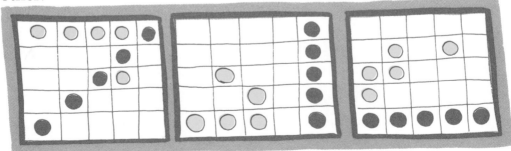

MENORAHS

1. Cut from construction paper a Chanukah menorah, leaving the center holder for the shamash candle a little higher. Cut out candles from multi-colored paper. The menorah can be stuck to a refrigerator or closet door with double-edged masking tape. Each night when Mother lights the real menorah, a child can light his own, by taping paper candles in their proper positions. This is a good idea for children too young to hold flaming candles and perfect for the child learning to count.

2. Collect empty wooden thread spools in three sizes. You will need nine large, ten medium, and nine small ones. Within each group they must be the same size. Ask an adult to cut you a wooden board 16 inches long and 2 or 3 inches wide. It will be the base of the menorah. Smooth it with sandpaper. Paint it in a bright color. Now paint each of the twenty-eight spools, using two or three colors that look well together, but only one color to a spool. One of the colors should be the same as that on the base. When spools and base are dry, start assembling the menorah. Use household cement. Attach the nine large spools to the base, spacing them evenly on the board. Let dry. To each of these spools, cement a medium-sized spool. Let dry. The middle candlestick will be the shamash. On that one, cement a second medium-sized spool to the one already in place. Let dry. On top of all nine candlesticks, cement the small spools. Let dry. These may now be decorated with beads, fancy buttons, Star of David cutouts from contact paper, or whatever else you may choose. For each candle, cut two collars with scalloped edges from 2-inch circles of foil. These will catch melting wax. Shave off ½ inch from the bottom of each Chanukah candle so it will fit into the spool hole. This can be done with a small knife or potato peeler. Each night of Chanukah, put a double foil collar on the candlesticks that will be lit, poke the candle through it, then press one piece of foil down and lift the other to form a cup. Your menorah is ready for lighting—right to left!

FOLD-DYE PAPERS

These are so simple a one-year-old child can help. And they are truly elegant! These papers do require the use of Japanese rice paper. Get the type known as Mulberry, which is available at art supply stores in sheets. Once completed they can be used in many ways—gift wrap, book covers, desk accessories, storage boxes, wall hangings, and whatever else you can think of.

Prepare cups of food coloring mixed with water in colors and hues of your choice. Cut sheets of rice paper to desired size. Fold each into a square, rectangle, or triangle shape. Dip one or more corners of the folded paper into the food coloring and mixes. Press out excess water and dye by placing the still-folded paper between two sheets of paper toweling which are between several sheets of newspaper. Step on it firmly. If you have young helpers, this is the part they love best!) Unfold the paper and lay it on newspaper to dry. The dyed papers must be handled carefully, for any water spots will spoil the design. To smooth out the creases, press the dry paper with a warm iron. (Don't use steam heat!)

PICTURE
YOURSELF

Friends and relatives would love a picture of you and your family, framed by you. Or they might enjoy a pretty picture cut from a magazine and framed.

1. *Mirror Pictures.* Take a small picture and glue it onto a handbag mirror. Fasten a small curtain ring to the back with strong cellophane or plastic tape for a hanger. The mirror itself will frame the picture.

2. *Tuna-can Pictures.* Ask an adult to remove the tops from three tuna cans, 2½ inches in diameter. Remove tuna and wash cans thoroughly, removing paper labels. Cut cardboard circles to fit bottom of cans. Choose small pictures for display. Using white glue, attach pictures to cardboard. Trim off rough edges of pictures. Glue to outside of cans. Join open ends with three paper clips, and you've got a triangle pyramid of pictures that stands alone.

ROCK PAPERWEIGHTS
OR DOORSTOPS

Select round, smooth stones for this project. Small ones can be used as paperweights; large ones as doorstops. Make sure they are clean and dry before painting. Poster paints, felt-tip pens, or acrylic paints can be used for the designs. If using poster paint, however, the paint will more readily stick to a stone's non-porous surface if the brush is rubbed over a cake of soap frequently while painting the design. For really bright colors, paint the stones white first. When dry, draw the design on stone with a pencil, then paint. For a shiny finish, coat with two coats of clear nail polish. Allow at least one hour between coats.

PENCIL HOLDER

Cut a strip of corrugated paper 1½ inches wide. The length you use will depend upon how large you want the holder to be. Use corrugated paper that has ribs showing on only one side; the type that has paper pasted over the ribs on both sides is too stiff. Roll the paper into a wheel, and hold it in place with cellophane tape or tie it up with cord. The outside of the roll may now be colored with paint or crayon or decorated with a pretty strip of patterned paper.

COBBLER APRON

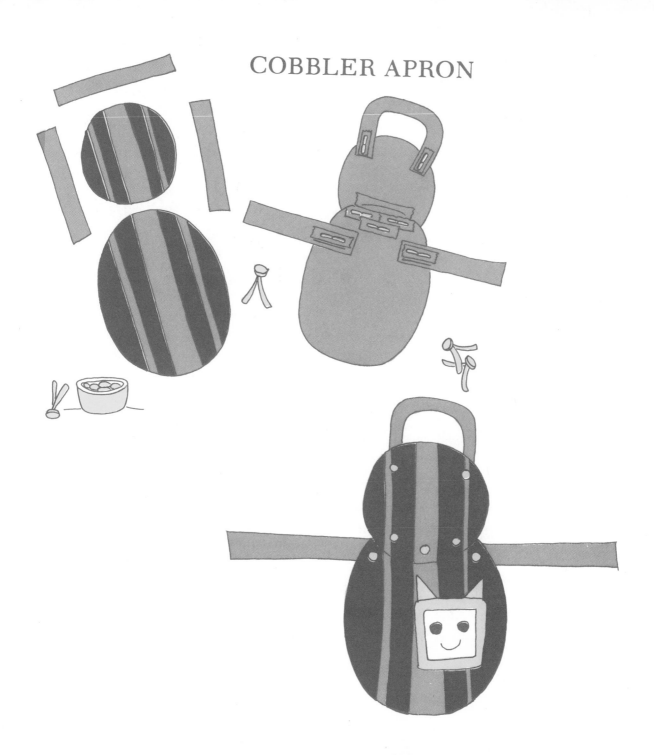

This apron will fit any young man or woman 40 to 55 inches tall, who likes to paint or work with tools.

Use vinyl cloth for this. Oilcloth, with or without a flannel backing, is good. The flannel backing makes a stronger apron, but it's a little more difficult to put holes in. You will also need self-sticking vinyl tape and round-head paper fasteners.

On the wrong side of the fabric, use a pencil to draw a 10-inch-wide circle for the bib. Then draw an 18-inch-long oval skirt. You can use a large dinner plate of the right size as a guide for the bib, and a tray or platter for the skirt. Cut out with either straight scissors or pinking shears, though the pinking edge is a fancier one. Place one edge of the bib over the skirt and tape together on the wrong side to hold in place. With straight scissors cut three strips 1 inch by 20 inches of the same or matching vinyl cloth for the neck strap and ties. To attach bib to skirt, punch a small hole with the point of a scissors through both pieces. Insert fasteners from front to back and secure in place, bib overlapping skirt. Do the same with the neck strap and ties, attaching the ties about 4 inches from where the bib and skirt meet. Cut out a pocket in the shape you want—fish, bird, triangle, square— and secure with fasteners as before. With vinyl tape, you may also outline the pocket and add a design, such as feet for the bird or an eye for the fish. On the wrong side of the apron, cover all ends of fasteners with cellophane or plastic tape to prevent their catching on clothes.

BIBS FOR BABY

1. Take twelve soft paper towels and cut out a half-circle, so they can fit around the neck. If desired, scallop the outside edges. Gently draw a design with felt-tip pens or crayons on each of the twelve towels. Put the twelve together and punch holes on each side of the neck with a paper punch or pencil. Cut a 30-inch length of ribbon in half so there will be two pieces, each 15 inches. Cut out a V-shape at all four ribbon ends to prevent unraveling. On each side of neck, insert one end of ribbon from back to front, through the holes, and knot it in front. As the sheets get soiled, they can be torn off, and the baby gets a new bib with a new design.

2. Another way of doing this is to use just six to eight pieces of toweling. Place pieces of waxed paper of the same size between each piece of toweling paper to prevent liquids from soaking through.

DREIDL GAME

Cut a piece of cardboard about 3 inches square. With pen or felt-tip marker draw one of the following Hebrew letters on each edge of the square.

NUN

HAY

GIMEL

SHIN

These letters are the initials for *Nes Gadol Hayah Sham*, which means "a great miracle happened there." Push a short pencil through the four-sided cardboard—and spin the *dreidl!*

The game is played with pennies, candies, or nuts, and any number can play. Each takes a turn spinning the dreidl. If it stops with *Nun* at the top, the player takes nothing from the pot. If *Gimel* is at the top, the player takes all; if *Hay*, the player gets half of the pot; if *Shin*, the player puts one nut or penny into the pot. The fame ends when one person has the whole pot. What a fun way to increase the amount of Chanukah *gelt!*

POTATO LATKES

Latkes are the most traditional of all Chanukah foods.

One story is that a woman named Judith fed the leader of the Maccabees' enemy lots of cheese to make him thirsty. He then drank too much wine and got drunk, making his capture possible. We sometimes eat cheese latkes to remind us of Judith's bravery. But in some countries many years ago, people could not get cheese in the wintertime, so potato latkes became very popular.

By some it is believed that the Maccabees ate latkes because they could be prepared quickly. Others think that the oil in which latkes are fried symbolizes the oil which burned for eight days. A meaningful history—and good tasting, too! They're always served during Chanukah festivities.

3 large potatoes	1 teaspoon salt
1 small onion	2 tablespoons flour
3 eggs	Vegetable oil for frying

1. Wash, pare, and grate raw potatoes. Strain.

2. Grate and add the onion.

3. Beat eggs well; add to potatoes.

4. Add salt and flour. Mix well.

5. Fry in frying pan, dropping carefully by spoonfuls into hot fat that is deep enough almost to cover the latkes. Turn only when underside is golden brown.

6. Fry on second side.

7. Drain on absorbent paper. Makes 18 pancakes. Serve with sour cream or applesauce.

Tu Bishevat

Tu Bishevat is known as the New Year for Trees, and is the beginning of spring in Israel. In Israel people celebrate by planting new trees. Where we live the ground is still too cold and hard for that, so, instead, we can grow different kinds of plants indoors. We can also eat the delicious fruits from trees in Israel—oranges, grapefruits, dates, pomegranates, figs, and carob fruit.

GROWING PLANTS

Don't expect big, glamorous houseplants. These are just fun projects and learning experiments. Any degree of success is fine.

1. An ordinary sweet potato will produce a beautiful vine. Suspend it by putting three or four toothpicks into the thick part of the potato. Then put the potato in a tall glass or jar so that the pointed tip is in water. Keep it in a sunny window. It takes about two weeks to sprout. As the vine starts to grow, tape a few strings up the window for the stems to climb on.

2. Grow an orchard! Save seeds from almost any common fruit—apple, pear, orange, grapefruit, lemon, orange. Dry the seeds on paper towels. Before planting, soak the seeds in water overnight. Place pebbles in the bottom of your planter for drainage. Add good potting soil to within a half inch of the top. Plant the seeds, keep soil moist, and wait for your pretty houseplant. When leaves appear, water only when surface of soil feels dry. Plants need good light—full sun isn't necessary.

3. An onion placed in a glass with the bottom half in water will produce interesting roots. Push three or four toothpicks into a center band around the onion. Fill glass with water. Put onion in glass with toothpicks resting on top to keep top half out of water. Roots develop first; eventually the top will sprout.

4. Cut off the bottoms of a carrot and stalk of celery. Soak them in water for an hour, then put them in a glass that contains a solution of food dye and water ($\frac{1}{2}$ teaspoon dye to $\frac{1}{2}$ cup water). Wait a day then cut the carrot in half lengthwise and the celery stalk crosswise to see how plants absorb moisture.

5. Grow a miniature forest by spreading a single layer of lentil beans over a saucer. Add enough water to moisten, but not float, the lentils. Keep moist and in a light place. After about ten days you will see little green stems and leaves. These little sprouts will grow for just a short time.

6. Cut off about 2 inches from the top of beets, turnips, carrots, or radishes. Trim off any leaves. Plant in a dish of pebbles with cut end down and add water. They'll grow quickly.

7. Take a small, fluffy sponge, the kind used for washing cars is best. Moisten it, and roll it in grass seed. Place it in a saucer of water in a bright, sunny window. Keep water in the saucer, and in a few days the sponge will be covered with a growth of green grass.

8. For a short-term experiment to watch how seeds grow from seed into plant, soak a piece of desk blotter in water. Wrap the wet blotter around the inside of a quart jar. Place fast-sprouting seeds such as peas or beans between the blotter and the glass. Put the lid on the jar. Wait for growth to start. When a leaf appears, loosen lid to let in air so mold won't form inside jar.

STUFFED DATES

Dates grow on palm trees in Israel.
These can be eaten like candy.

> ¾ cup pitted dates
> About 21 miniature marshmallows or
> ¼ cup walnut or pecan halves
> Flaked coconut or confectioners' sugar

Stuff each date with a marshmallow or a nut. Roll in coconut
or confectioners' sugar.

✋ TREE PLAQUE

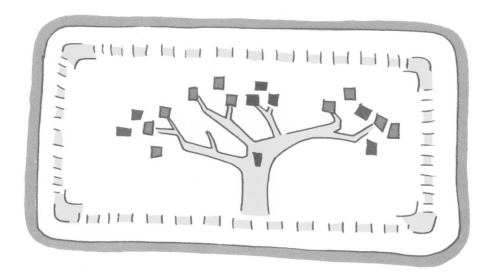

White plastic foam meat trays are terrific for crafts projects. For a starter, try a tree plaque for Tu Bishevat. Draw a bare tree on the bottom of one of these trays with a black or brown permanent ink felt-tip pen. Cut small squares or leaf-shapes from two shades of green construction paper. Glue each one onto the tree, just as if spring had arrived and the tree had grown new leaves. These trees can hold a great many leaves, becoming three dimensional.

Many types of paper pictures can be mounted on the bottom of these meat-tray frames. Because they are so lightweight, one or two pieces of doubled-over masking tape will hold them to a wall.

TREES

1. Give each player a pencil and a piece of paper on the top of which has been printed the word POMEGRANATES. They are well-known trees that grow in Israel with a red fruit the size of an orange. At a given signal each player writes as many words as he can find jumbled up in POMEGRANATES. The first one with ten correct words is the winner.

2. At a given signal, on the other side of the paper, have each player list as many names of trees as possible. Set a time limit for this. When time is up, the one with the longest list of trees is the winner.

Purim

The happiest and noisiest Jewish holiday is Purim. There are parties and plays, Purim songs and costume parades, and lots of *hamantashen*, those delicious, triangular little cakes. Sometimes, gifts are given to friends—that's called *schlach manot*—or money is given to people in need. The story of Queen Esther and wicked Haman, called the Megillah, is read aloud in the synagogue. A long, long time ago, the country of Persia was ruled by King Ahasuerus. One of the men in his kingdom was Haman. He was a very, very mean man. Esther was the king's wife at this time. She is the heroine in the Purim story. Esther, with the help of her cousin Mordecai, protected their people, the Jews, from those that were trying to hurt them. When the name "Haman" is read in the synagogue, children stamp their feet and whirl or bang their noisemakers, called *graggers,* so no one can hear his name. The children dress up like characters in the story, and prizes are given for the best costumes. At Purim parties there are always *hamantashen,* so called because they are shaped like Haman's hat.

PURIM BALLOONS

Decorate a holiday home with painted balloons. Use poster paints to decorate blown-up balloons with the faces of Purim characters. Keep the mouthpiece at the top of the head since it will be covered by hair or hat. Glue or tape on pieces of paper for hair, eyes, mouth, beard, hats, and crowns. Remember there are many types of paper—crepe, construction, and foil, to mention just a few. You can also use shiny gift wrap ribbon for hair. It can be curled at the end by putting ribbon between thumb and opened scissor blade. Pull the blade along the length of ribbon and the end should curl. Cotton, too, is good for beards or mustaches or hair. Hang the balloons with string or ribbons—singly or in clusters.

MUMBLE JUMBLE

Give a list of jumbled words found below in the first column to each of the players. They must write the correct word next to the jumbled one. Allow ten minutes for the game. The one who has the largest number of correct words wins. The answers are here, too, but don't let anyone else see them!

Jumbled Words	*Answers*
LACHSCH TAMON	SCHLACH MANOT
MANAHNEHATS	HAMANTASHEN
DEARMICO	MORDECAI
SHAUERUSA	AHASUERUS
THERES	ESTHER
NHAAM	HAMAN
GILLHAME	MEGILLAH
ERGGARG	GRAGGER
IMPRU	PURIM

GRAGGERS

1. Crayon or paint designs on a small box. Put in a handful of beans or raw popcorn and tape the two halves of the box together, using plain cellophane tape or a more colorful plastic or cloth tape.

2. Or make this gragger from a frozen juice can from which one lid has been neatly removed. Empty the can, wash, and dry it. Carefully punch two holes in the other lid of the can with a hammer and nail. An adult can do that for you. Cover the sides with colored paper, using glue or cellophane tape. You can draw a Purim symbol on it. With string, tie screws or metal washers to the center of a pipe cleaner. Then poke the ends of the pipe cleaner through the two holes at the top of the can. Twist the ends together to form a handle.

HIT HAMAN

This is a game most often played at Purim carnivals but which can easily be played in the home. Either bean bags or soft balls can be used.

Take a large piece of cardboard and draw a picture of Haman on it. Cut out an open mouth, a nose, and two eyes, in graduated sizes. Make the mouth the largest and the eyes smallest. Be sure that all the holes are large enough for the bags or balls to pass through. Next to each opening write in point values: 5 for the mouth; 10 for the nose; 20 for the eyes. Lean the head against a wall at a good angle for the bean bags to go into the holes. Prop it up with a heavy book at its base, in front, to prevent sliding. Give each player a bean bag or two or three, in turn, and watch him total up his points. First one to reach 75 wins the game!

HAMANTASHEN

2½ cups flour
1 tablespoon baking powder
1 teaspoon salt
¼ cup sugar
¾ cup milk or water

1 egg, beaten
⅓ cup butter
Prune, poppy seed or
   apricot pie filling
1 egg yolk

94

1. Heat oven to 350° F.

2. Sift together the flour, baking powder, and salt. Stir in the sugar. Make a well in the center of the flour and pour in milk or water and beaten egg.

3. Melt butter; cool; pour into center of flour.

4. Stir together to make a dough that is soft but not sticky. Knead five or six times on a floured board. (How to knead is explained on page 17.) Roll out to ⅛-inch thickness.

5. Cut into 3½- to 4-inch circles with a drinking glass whose rim has been dipped in flour. Place a half teaspoonful of filling in the center of each round. Draw up three sides to the center to form a triangle. Pinch edges together.

6. Arrange well apart on a greased cookie sheet. Brush tops with the egg yolk, thinned with a little water. The water makes it easier to apply.

7. Bake for 15 to 20 minutes or until hamantashen are golden brown. Makes about 30.

GINGERBREAD
QUEEN ESTHER AND HAMAN

For the dough, it's easiest to buy a package of gingerbread mix and follow the directions on the box for rolled cookies. Cut simple patterns from 4-by-6-inch index cards. After the dough is rolled out, place patterns on it and, with a knife, cut around the edges. Or use boy and girl cookie cutters. Press in raisin eyes, a gumdrop mouth, and a red cinnamon candy nose. Extra trimmings can be red cinnamon drops, raisins, chopped nuts, candied cherries, cut-up gumdrops, tiny silver candies, colored coconut flakes.

After the cookies are baked, you can decorate with frosting, too. Again, the easiest kind to use is the one that comes in tubes and is sold in supermarkets, along with decorative tips. Use different colors and tips for variety.

You don't really have to limit your cookies to Queen Esther and Haman. With the same two patterns, try making others in the Megillah story—Queen Vashti, King Ahasuerus, and Mordecai.

COSTUMES FOR
QUEEN ESTHER AND HAMAN

1. *Earrings.* Earrings can be made with string loops that fit over your ears. Wrap or tie beads, tin foil balls, marbles, small shells, and paper cutouts with string and attach to the loops.

2. *Wood Bracelet.* Soak a tongue depressor in water until it can be bent. Bend it and place around the inside of a small drinking glass. Let dry. Decorate with crayons or paint, or glue on beads.

3. *Plastic Jewelry.* With strong scissors (not the small children's type), cut plastic pieces from small, empty, and well-washed bleach bottles. Decorate with plastic or cloth tape. Circles will make bracelets; odd shapes, pins or medals that can be "pinned" to clothing with double-edged masking tape.

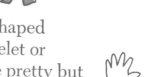

4. *Colorful Necklaces and Bracelets.* String odd-shaped pieces of macaroni on a shoelace for a pretty bracelet or necklace. The macaroni can be painted. These are pretty but fragile. String colored beads and buttons the same way.

Pretty necklaces can be made from paper and plastic straws cut in 1-inch lengths. Also use 1-inch squares or circles of colored paper with small holes cut or poked in the center. These can be strung alternately with the straws on a shoelace. Shoelaces are best for this because they are safe and easy to handle.

5. *Haman's Hat.* From drawing paper or a large grocery bag, cut out a circle 12 inches wide. Cut a circle out of the center large enough to fit your head. Color or paint the brim on both sides of the paper, then fold it into a triangular shape to make the three-cornered hat.

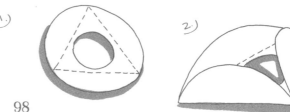

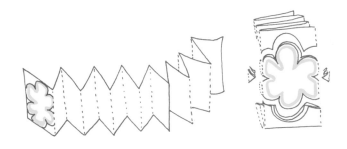

6. *Queen Esther's Crown*. Cut a piece of paper 24 inches long and 4 inches wide. Fold it back and forth, accordion-style. Make each pleat about 1¼ inches wide. On the top pleat, draw the outline of a flower as illustrated. Cut along the outline through all thicknesses. Be sure that paper on both the right and left sides of the picture remains uncut. Open up the pleats for a very pretty floral crown. Color the flowers with crayons or felt-tip pens. Fit crown around head for correct size and tape ends together.

MASKS

Because happiness and fun are part of Purim, plays have
been traditional for this holiday for hundreds of years. You
can put on a play about the Megillah's tale of Queen Esther
using these masks. They are quite simple to make:

1. *Tie-on Masks*. Cut a mask shape from construction paper
large enough to cover your face. To the sides attach strings

long enough to tie behind the head. They can be stapled to
the sides or tied through holes. Draw in eyes, nose, and
mouth, then cut them out with scissors. Decorate the mask
as you please.

A stiffer mask can be made from a paper plate. Staple on
elastic (available in fabric stores or dime stores), cut long
enough so it can slip over your head. Cut out holes for eyes
and nose. Now decorate the plate. This is a better mask than
the paper one because the plate won't rip as easily and you
can put it on and take it off by yourself.

Extra touches can be added to the masks: cotton for beards
and mustaches; ribbons, yarn, or crepe paper streamers for
hair; fringed construction paper for eyelashes; felt for
eyebrows. Apply with tape or glue.

2. *Paper Bag Masks.* An ordinary brown paper bag makes a great mask!

Cut holes for eyes, nose, and mouth (any shape desired). If a large grocery bag is being used, cut armholes, too. (Ask Mother if she can get the long *paper* bags used in some laundries. They're even better if you are tall. Unfortunately, they're now very hard to find.) Make armholes in an oval shape. Cover edges with cellophane tape to prevent rips. You'll need glue, scraps of yarn, bits of cotton, paints or crayons or felt-tip pens, and construction paper. The paper bags are high enough to make crowns for Ahasuerus or Esther masks. Draw them on the bags or add an extra piece of construction paper. Glue on glass beads or fancy buttons for crown jewels. For other decorating ideas, see Tie-on Masks, page 100.

Passover

Passover is a festival of freedom. Houses get a special cleaning; everything sparkles and shines. There is a family ceremony called a Seder—when we read from the Haggadah, a book that tells the Passover story. Everybody reads a part of this, and the youngest child asks four questions about why this night is so special. At the head of the table where Father sits is a matzo cloth containing three pockets for three whole matzos; the Seder plate with a roasted lamb bone, a roasted egg, horseradish, parsley, and *charoses*, a mixture of apples, nuts, cinnamon, and wine; a bowl of salt water; and a bottle of wine. They tell the story of Passover, too. There is also a large wine cup, the cup for the prophet Elijah. In some families. Father hides a piece of matzo that is called the *afikomen*. If the children can find it, Father has to give them a reward for returning it. Passover lasts for one whole week. That's eight days of matzos and special foods, holiday games and songs.

MATZO COVER

This can be used at the Seder table.

A piece of white cotton cloth is required. Cut the fabric with a pinking shears to prevent it from unraveling. The finished piece should measure 8 inches by 32 inches. Fold the cut cloth, accordion-style, into four sections. You will have formed three "pockets" for each of three pieces of matzo. Draw a picture or design that is suitable for Passover on the top fold of the cloth. Use permanent ink felt-tip marking pens so that the colors will not wash out.

BOOKMARKS FOR HAGGADAH

 1. These are so easy to do, you can make one for every guest at the Seder. Cut off the corner of an envelope for each bookmark. Decorate with crayons or felt-tip pens. To use, just slip it over the corner of the page.

2. Select a long animal such as an alligator, dog, or caterpillar. Make each bookmark about 9 inches long. Cut out colored rectangles or other shapes of felt. With glue attach each piece to an 8-inch length of baby rickrack. Then, gluing felt to felt, add eyes, spots, ears, antenna, or whatever else the animal requires.

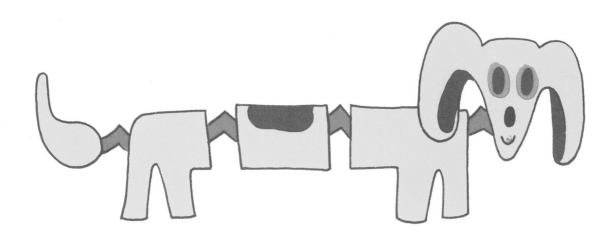

WHAT AM I?

Pin on the back of each player the name or picture of some of the Passover objects, places, or characters. Each person must then find out who or what he is by questioning others. He can only ask questions that can be answered by yes or no. Examples are: Am I useful? Am I good to eat? Am I a place? As soon as the person guesses what he is, the picture can be removed from his back and pinned to the front of his clothing.

Here are several ideas:

HAGGADAH	PHARAOH	ROASTED EGG	MOSES
RED SEA	CHAROSES	PROPHET ELIJAH	MATZO
FOUR QUESTIONS	FOUR SONS	AN ONLY KID	AFIKOMEN

AN ONLY KID

This is "An Only Kid" as in "*Chad Gadya*," the song about the little goat that Father bought for two coins.

1. Draw and cut out the shape of a little goat from lightweight cardboard. Cover the board with white glue. For the "furry" look, press popcorn, excelsior, or dry cereals onto the glue. Let dry. This can be hung on the wall with adhesive picture mounts, available at dime stores.

2. Or draw a picture of a little goat on a piece of heavier cardboard or plywood. Cover the goat with white glue. Then cover with colored aquarium gravel. Let the glue dry, then shake the extra gravel off. In a color different from the goat, fill in the background to the edges following the same pattern—cover with glue, then cover with gravel. Let the glue dry, then shake the extra gravel off. This makes a decorative picture for the holidays. Heavy cardboard can be hung with adhesive picture mounts. Plywood, because of its weight, will require something stronger like mirror hangers, available in hardware stores.

✋ FEEL AND TELL BOX

Play a game of sensory perception with a surprise box that all children will love. With a scissors, cut a hole in one end of a box. A shoe box works well. Cut the cuff off a man's sock. With strong tape (plastic tape is good), tape the cuff around the hole so children can slide their hands through the cuff to feel various objects with interesting textures. Hinge the lid with tape and tie shut to prevent peeking. You will need objects large enough for the children to grasp, yet small enough to fit easily in the box. For example: a small piece of matzo, a hard-boiled egg (still in the shell), a candle, wine cup, Jewish star, or nuts.

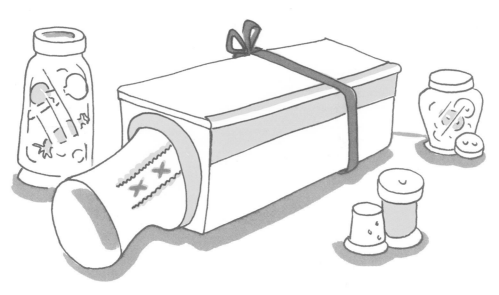

PASSOVER JAM PUFFS

¼ cup shortening
½ cup boiling water
½ cup sifted matzo meal
⅛ teaspoon salt

2 eggs
Vegetable oil for frying
Cherry or raspberry jam
Powdered sugar, if desired

1. Bring shortening and water to a boil in a saucepan. Lower heat. Mix matzo meal with salt and add to mixture in saucepan. Beat vigorously until mixture is thick and separates easily from sides of the pan. Remove from heat.

2. In the same saucepan, add eggs, beating in vigorously one at a time, until entire mixture is smooth and thoroughly blended.

3. In another saucepan containing hot fat about ½ inch deep, drop level teaspoons of the mixture and fry until lightly browned on all sides. Hot oil may spatter when you do this—please be careful.

4. Remove puffs with slotted spoon and drain on absorbent paper. Cool.

5. Slit puffs on top and insert a small amount of jam in each. Sprinkle with powdered sugar, if desired. Makes 25 to 30 puffs.

Israel Independence Day

On May 14, 1948, the State of Israel came into being. This opened a home for Jews from all over the world. Jews had waited many long years for this, and when the day finally came, everyone was very happy. This special day is celebrated as a holiday by people in Israel and by their friends everywhere.

ISRAELI FLAG

From a piece of light blue construction paper, cut two strips, 1 inch by 11 inches. Cut a Star of David the same color. Glue these to a piece of white construction paper to form the Israeli flag. Glue or staple the flag to a narrow dowel or twig.

STAR OF DAVID

You'll need ice cream or craft sticks for this. They can be bought at hobby shops or dime stores.

To make a six-pointed star, glue three ice cream sticks together to form a triangle with ends overlapping. Glue three more sticks together to form a second triangle. Glue this on top of the first one to form a Star of David. Put a string through the top to make a pendant necklace, or keep building until there are three or four layers. If desired, paint with acrylics or tempera. This second, thicker star may be hung, used as the base of a floral centerpiece, or filled to overflowing with little cupcakes or Israeli fruits.

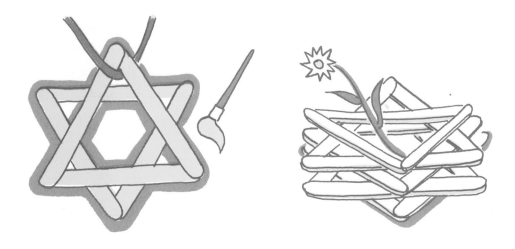

PEBBLE ART

Collect a pailful of assorted size pebbles. Decide on your colors and your design—perhaps an Israeli flag or a seven-branched menorah like the one in Jerusalem. Keep it simple.

Paint the pebbles in different colors with acrylic paint—only the side that will show on the mosaic. Lay them on a newspaper to dry. On a plywood board, draw your design. Mark the colors needed in each area. Using household cement, glue the pebbles to the board one at a time. Work with one color at a time. It will be easier if you start in the middle and work toward the outside edges. Let the glue dry overnight. Tap very gently on the board on the other side. If any pebbles come off, just glue them back to their positions on the board and let dry again. If there are any gaps on the board, take the same color paint for that area and just paint the gaps. Let dry. For a shiny finish, apply a coat of Mod Podge.

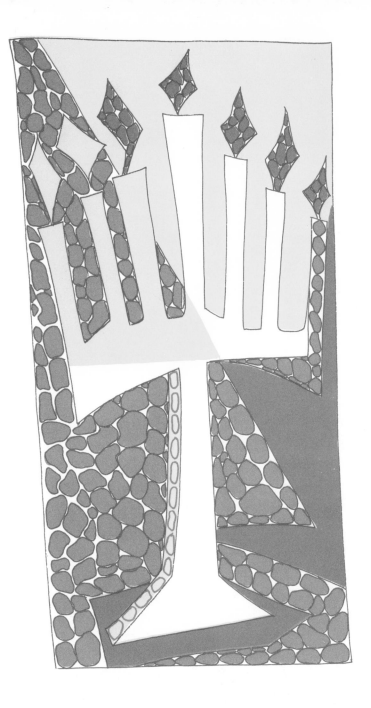

EMBROIDERED FLOWERS
OF ISRAEL

Here are some of the flowers of Israel:

Iris	Cornflower	Oleander	Daffodil	Trident
Peony	Buttercup	Anemone	Cyclamen	Orchid
				Tulip

Identify each in a seed catalog to see how it looks.

Now, plan your design for a burlap picture using one or more of the flowers. Start with a piece of heavy paper. Make it the same size you want your finished picture to be. Draw your picture on the paper. Cut around the flower outline. Trace around the design onto the burlap with felt-tip pens. For the finishing touches, use pieces of colored yarn. For each flower use the same color yarn as the color of the marking pen. The pieces of yarn should be no longer than the length of your arm, otherwise they get tangled. Thread a blunt-nosed embroidery needle with a piece of yarn. Tie a knot in the long end.

You can now embroider each of the flowers on your picture. For this you will need to know two basic stitches:

The first is the running stitch. This is a small stitch. You make it by running the needle in and out of the burlap in a straight line. The length of the stitches and the space between them should be the same.

The second is the backstitch. Take a stitch back and bring the needle forward the length of one stitch from where you started. Now make another backstitch, meeting the last stitch, and bring the needle forward one stitch.

Always start on the back, so your knots won't be seen. As you finish with each piece of yarn, pull it through to the back side again. Slide the needle under two or three of the stitches in the back to lock yarn in. Cut off the leftover yarn with a scissor. If the burlap has wrinkled up while embroidering, it will be necessary to iron it flat with a warm iron. For hanging your picture, see page 121.

FALAFEL

1 20-ounce can chick peas,
  drained
½ teaspoon garlic powder
2 tablespoons cornstarch
1 egg, beaten
½ teaspoon baking soda

¾ teaspoon salt
¼ teaspoon chili powder
2 tablespoons chopped parsley
1 tablespoon vegetable oil
Vegetable oil for deep frying

1. Mash the chick peas well in a medium-sized bowl.

2. Mix in garlic powder, cornstarch, egg, baking soda, salt, chili powder, parsley, and vegetable oil. Let stand 10 minutes.

3. Heat about 3 inches of oil in deep pot. Carefully drop *falafel* mixture by teaspoonfuls into hot oil. Fry about 3 minutes or until golden brown. The little balls will rise to the top. Drain on paper towels. Makes about 24.

ISRAELI VEGETABLE SALAD

½ tomato
¼ green pepper
½ carrot
½ cucumber

5 radishes
1 tablespoon salad oil
1 tablespoon lemon juice
salt and pepper to taste

Cut each of the vegetables into small pieces. Put in medium-sized bowl. Add oil, lemon, salt and pepper. Mix well. Refrigerate until ready to use. Makes about 2 cups.

In Israel falafel is traditionally served in *pita*—a flat, hollow bread available in some supermarkets and specialty stores. Open the pita, fill with falafel, and spoon on salad over the top. Or serve it plain, without the pita, and with this salad on the side. Good for lunch!

HANGING BURLAP PICTURES

Cut two dowel sticks about 2 inches longer than the width of your picture. Glue or staple the burlap to the back of the dowels. If you prefer, you may sew two "pockets" for the dowels at the top and bottom. Be sure each is large enough for the dowel to slide through. Do top and bottom in the same way. Fold over the burlap, so that the edges are at the back of your picture. Using either a running stitch or a backstitch, sew both pieces of burlap together with yarn. Slide the dowels through. At the top, tie a piece of colored yarn from one side of the dowel to the other. Your burlap picture will hang from that—as a bright spot on your bedroom wall!

Lag Ba'Omer

This is the only outdoor holiday in our Jewish calendar. Ever since the days when Jewish scholars went into the forest dressed as hunters to fool their Roman enemies, Jewish children have celebrated Lag Ba'Omer.

In Israel children go into the woods and fields dressed as hunters for a day of fun. Here we go on picnics. We hear stories about Rabbi Akiba, a very wise teacher, and about Bar Kochba, a brave soldier, who lived a long time ago. Children shoot bows and arrows, run relay races, and play many outdoor games.

⠘ BOATS OR BARGES

For that Lag Ba'Omer picnic, boats are great fun . . . especially when you can build your own. Milk cartons are all you need.

1. For a sailboat, stick the pointed end of a pencil through the top side of an empty carton. Tape a triangle of colored paper to the pencil. Attach a string to one end, so the boat doesn't get away from you.

2. If you prefer a string of barges, cut away one side of several cartons and push out the ends to form bows. Join the barges, bow to stern, with string.

ACTION RELAY

To start, the players should stand in line one behind the other with four to eight players on a team, each equal in number. The first member of each team stands just behind the starting line. Teams stand parallel to each other about 3 feet apart. In a relay race only the first person on each team starts at the signal "go." He does whatever action is required and returns to his team. He touches the right hand of the second person on his team, then goes to the end of his line. When everyone has had a turn he becomes first again. The first team to finish all the relays raises their hands to signal they have won.

The following can be used in any number of combinations: everyone can have four turns to complete all actions, each player can do a different action, the players may hop up and skip back or run up and hop back.

> hopping on one foot to and around a tree
> jumping on both feet to and around a tree
> skipping to and around a tree
> running to and around a tree

Different actions may be used in endless combinations.

TARGET TOSS

You can be just like Bar Kochba's soldiers, who practiced hitting targets when they were dressed as huntsmen.

Take an empty egg carton and tear off the top. With felt-tip pens or paint, write a number from one to twelve inside each egg cup. Give each player six "arrows"—buttons, pennies, large beans, or bottle tops. Let each player take a turn at tossing his arrows into the cups. He totals up his score by the point value of the cup where his arrow lands. Whoever gets fifty points first is the winner.

How far the players stand from the target depends on their age. Young "archers" can play this game with older players, but they should be allowed to stand closer to the target.

BOX LUNCH

This is handy for a Lag Ba'Omer picnic!

Fill each compartment of an egg carton with finger food: lunch meat roll-ups, hard-cooked egg wedges, cheese cubes, carrot sticks, pineapple cubes, fresh strawberries, cookies. Close the carton and tie with a pretty piece of ribbon or yarn.

For a really special "box"—decorate the egg carton. Glued on paper flowers or flowers cut from adhesive-backed contact paper will cover any writing on the carton and brighten up your lunch box for your box lunch!

Shavuot

On Shavuot we celebrate three things. It was on this day many, many years ago that the Jewish people were given the Ten Commandments. For this honor we decorate the synagogue with flowers, because the Torah is in the synagogue and in the Torah are written the Ten Commandments. Shavuot is also a harvest festival, for in Israel this is the time when the wheat is gathered. It is also when the first fruits begin to ripen, and children bring some of these fruits to the synagogue. In many synagogues this is when confirmations are held, when children graduate from religious school.

FLOWER FANCIES

Shavuot is a springtime holiday. Fill the house with flowers!

1. *Wire Flowers.* For each flower cut 8-inch lengths of plastic bell wire (it's also called electronic wire) in assorted colors. Bend the wire to form flowers and leaves. Try coiling the wire, twisting it around a pencil, or just bending it for the different flower shapes. Use 5- or 10-inch lengths for stems. Twist the stem around the flower center. Put a hunk of clay into a colorful paper cup, then stick the free end of the stem into this. For the long-stemmed variety, it may be necessary to add a few stones to the cup so it won't tip over.

2. *Paper Daisies*. Cut two 3¼-inch circles for each flower from adhesive-backed contact paper, either printed or plain. Some wide-mouth drinking glasses are about that size. You could use one for drawing the circle pattern. Put the two circles together and cut them again into a five-petal daisy. Peel off the backing on one flower. Lay a thin, soft wire, 8 inches long, on the sticky side with the top point in the center of flower. Use green floral wire, if possible. It can be cut easily with a scissor. Then leaving the backing on the second flower, carefully place it over the sticky side of the first flower and press it down firmly. All outside edges should be together. Any little mistakes can be trimmed away with a scissor. Cut out two 1¼-inch circles in another paper for centers. The size of a quarter will do. Peel off sticky backing and press in place. If you use a plain paper for the flower, use a printed center; if a printed flower, a plain center. You've made a stiff-petaled blossom that can be curved. Repeat each step for every flower. Cover a juice can with the same printed contact paper. Stick the wire ends of the flowers into a piece of styrofoam or clay in the bottom of the can. When flowers are arranged, fill can with pretty stones, marbles, or crushed tissue paper.

EGGSHELL BASKET

Start with half a plastic egg—the kind that is sold in supermarkets and drugstores as packaging for ladies' stockings. Decorate the outside by gluing on bits of paper or strips of fancy ribbon. For hanging, tape on a handle of string or ribbon. If you prefer that the egg stand upright, cut a strip of construction paper 5½ inches long and ¾ inch wide. Overlap the edges and tape closed. This will be the egg stand.

Fill the basket with small flowers—either real or dried or artificial.

CHEESE CARTON
FLOWER POT

Use a clean, dry cottage cheese carton or a clean, empty
coffee or peanut can. Apply construction paper, contact
paper, yarn, or twine around the outside. The yarn or twine
may be glued onto the carton by winding either around
and around the side of the can. A little glue will hold the
end of the twine at the bottom. When you reach the top,
fasten the other end of the twine with glue and hold it
in place with a clothespin till the glue dries. A coat of
Mod Podge over the whole thing will give the flower
pot a shiny look.

The cheese carton flower pot will hold any of the flowers
listed in this book, but it is also perfect for a real houseplant.

HANGING MOBILE

Cut a strip of cardboard or heavy paper 3 or 4 inches wide and about 24 inches long. Glue or tape the ends together to make a circle. From construction paper cut and decorate holiday items. For Shavuot—fruits, flowers, the Torah, the Ten Commandments stone, Stars of David, candlesticks, a synagogue. Make a small hole at the top of each shape. Use a hole puncher or sharp point of a pencil. Make holes around the bottom edge of the cardboard circle. Pull pieces of string through the holes in the decorations and hang them from the holes in the circle. Make four holes in the top of the circle and attach strings for hanging. Hang the mobile from a light fixture or in an open doorway.

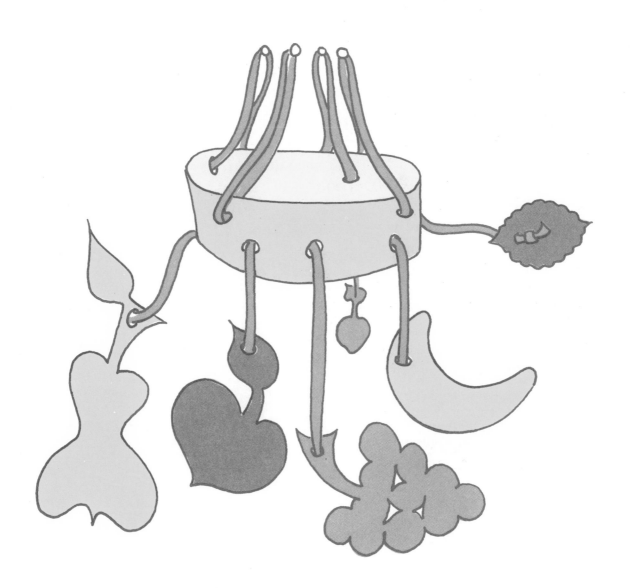

MOSES AND THE
TEN COMMANDMENTS

Start with a clean empty 1-pound coffee can. Cover it with white paper. Glue on eyes and nose cut from colored paper or felt. Cut hair from white paper. Glue hair at top of cylinder or shape absorbent cotton as hair and glue. Cut beard and mustache. Glue under nose, or use cotton again for both. Cut eyebrows of paper or cotton. Glue them on. Cut an arm piece long enough to go around the cylinder with room to spare. From heavier paper cut a Ten Commandments stone. Glue hands over it.

MEMORY LOTTO

For each player, cut a piece of colored construction paper so it measures 6 inches wide and 9 inches high. Using a ruler, mark off six 3-inch-square boxes on each sheet. From a magazine, seed package, or flower catalogue, cut out six pictures of fruits and flowers for each lotto card. You will need two copies of each picture. Trim to fit and glue them down within the ruled lines. If the pictures are too difficult to find, draw the objects in the squares. Cut out six 3-inch squares for each player. On these individual squares, glue one small picture to match every picture on the larger lotto card. As an example, for four players, you will need twenty-four different pictures in duplicate. Mix the small squares and place them in a paper bag.

To play, have everyone sit in a circle. Place one lotto card, face down, in front of each player. Explain that no one may look at his card until you give the signal. When you say "Go!" each player may turn his card over and memorize the pictures on the card and the positions of these pictures. After about one minute, tell the players to turn the cards face down again and sit on them. Now—hold up one small card at a time. Whoever remembers having that card may ask for it and must place it on the floor in front of him. As the players add several cards, they must try to arrange them to look like their original large card. The first player to arrange six cards in perfect order is the winner.

CHEESE SQUARES

Heat oven to 350° F.

For the crust, mix together:

> 1¼ cups graham cracker crumbs
> ¼ cup sugar
> ¼ cup butter or margarine, melted

Press with a spatula or wooden spoon into the bottom of an 8-inch-square pan.

For the filling:

1 pound cottage cheese
4 oz. cream cheese,
   at room temperature
¾ cup sugar
1 teaspoon vanilla

2 eggs
1 5-oz. can evaporated milk
2 tablespoons flour
1 tablespoon lemon juice

Combine all ingredients and mix with a beater. Pour over the cracker crumb crust in the square pan. Sprinkle the top with extra graham cracker crumbs. Bake for 45 minutes.

INDEX

WENDY PHILLIPS LAZAR was born in Rochester, New York, and graduated from Syracuse University with a degree in Radio-Television and Elementary Education. Her career in educational broadcasting includes three years in television as a producer, writer, and hostess of a weekly interview program, and seven years in radio as a producer, director, writer and on-air personality both in the United States and Japan. Ms. Lazar and her husband, a psychiatric social worker and therapist, live with their two children in Closter, New Jersey.

MARION BEHR won her first award for book illustration in a statewide contest at the age of seven and has been drawing ever since. A graduate of Syracuse University with a B.F.A. in Art Education and M.F.A. in Painting, she has exhibited her paintings and sculptures in galleries in New Jersey and New York. Her illustrations, craft projects, and toy designs have been featured in many national magazines. Ms. Behr lives in Edison, New Jersey, with her husband, a patent attorney, and three children.